The Road
Where the People Cried
Nunna da-ul Tsun-yi

MONGREL EMPIRE PRESS
NORMAN, OKLAHOMA, UNITED STATES OF AMERICA

2020

Acknowledgments

Some of these poems have previously appeared elsewhere. The author gratefully acknowledges permission to reprint by the editors of *The Clouds Threw This Light: Contemporary Native American Poetry* (Institute of American Indian Arts Press), *Southwest: A Contemporary Anthology* (Red Earth Press), and the book, *Deer Hunting and Other Poems* (Point Riders Press/Contact/ II Publications).

Praise for *The Road Where the People Cried*

Geary Hobson uses the power of narrative to re-walk the Trail of Tears. His collection of voices traces the forced march, sickness, upheaval and dispossession of the Cherokee removal. Rain Crow, Dragging Canoe, White Path, Pigeon Woman, Richard Old Field, George Lowrey, Dreadfulwater, Jesse Bushyhead are a few of the speakers who illuminate "one of the worst blemishes on American history." But it is Hobson's own "cross-cut saw" of words that makes *The Road Where the People Cried* remarkable.

—Diane Glancy, author of
Pushing the Bear and The Book of Bearings

Geary Hobson's *The Road Where the People Cried* brings both the human tragedy and legal travesty of Cherokee Removal to life for today's readers through the historical figures who voice his vivid and compelling poetry. From Six Killer to Tsali to Dragging Canoe and even the vile, sorry, low down, no good, ne'er do well Andrew Jackson, these characters will make you sit down and listen.

—Kimberly G. Wieser, author of
Texas… to Get Horses and *Back to the Blanket:
Recovered Rhetorics and Literacies in American Indian Studies*

In his eighties by then, Going Snake saw what life had become for his Indigenous people when they were forced to leave their homelands. He saw and felt their sorrow and loss. He heard and suffered their cries and pain. Nevertheless, he knew and insisted on this truth: Life-Everlasting. This is the deeper, fiercer, and loving core of Nunna da-ul Tsun-yi. *The Road Where the People Cried*. This is the love deep and everlasting. Ever Lasting. Ever. Lasting. These poems by Geary Hobson must be read.

—Simon J. Ortiz, author of
*Speaking for the Generations, Out There Somewhere,
Going for the Rain, Beyond the Reach of Time and Change,
The Good Rainbow Road, From Sand Creek*, and many more.

FIRST EDITION, 2020

The Road Where the People Cried
© 2020 by Geary Hobson

ISBN 978-1-7323935-3-0

Cover Art
One Last Look by Janet Lamon Smith
©2019

Author Photo
@2018 by Sharon Lee

MONGREL EMPIRE PRESS
NORMAN, OK

Online catalogue: www.mongrelempire.org

This publisher is a proud member of

[clmp]

COUNCIL OF LITERARY MAGAZINES & PRESSES
w w w . c l m p . o r g

Contents

For the Cherokees
Now, Then, and Always

Prologue

With the end of the American Revolution and for nearly fifty years afterwards, white Americans on the frontier clamored for the liquidation of all Indian lands east of the Mississippi River. Treaty after treaty was enacted with the tribes residing there, whose attachment to their ancestral lands was not less dearly held by them than the westward-moving whites and perhaps even more so. Creeks, Chickasaws, Choctaws, Seminoles, and Cherokees were the big ones in the South, and Kickapoos, Shawnees, Delawares, Miamis, Sac and Foxes, and a score or so more in the North — all of which bore strong attachments to their ancestral lands — were subjected to the treaty-making process. Hopewell, Hard Labor, Dancing Rabbit Creek, Payne's Landing, Pontotoc, New Echota — these are only a few of the now all-but-forgotten names of treaty sites, each of which marked an additional step in the disintegrating Indian domain, each representing a little more of the whittling away of the Tree of Nation for Indian people. Soon the Tree was all but gone in the old lands, the various chips and cuttings swept westward into the lands the white man designated as Indian Territory or into out of the way fastnesses of swamps and mountains of their homeland or into the hide-in-plain-sight existences of fringe living in the white man's towns and communities, often successfully disguised as off-whites not only to whites, but often to themselves as the years went by. Indian Territory, or as the Choctaw word "Oglahomma" — Red Man's Land — defined it, was to be the new Tree of

Nation. However, enclaves of Indian people remain in isolated pockets throughout the lands east of the Mississippi River—like splintered chips, or even sawdust—after the implacable movement of the white Christian American English-speaking steel cross-cut saw had worked its way through the native wood.

The Indians would have to move, so felt most whites in the first three decades of the nineteenth century. However, it was not until the inauguration of Andrew Jackson as the seventh president of the United States in 1829 that Indian removal became formally established as federal policy. Jackson—*Tsek-sani*, or Old Chicken Snake, *Skey-no-yain-eh*—as the Cherokees called him, was deeply committed to removing the tribes. What happened in the next decade and a half—the bribery, chicanery, fraudulent treaties, wars, round-ups, incarceration in concentration camps (and yes, the term concentration camp, coined by General Winfield Scott, was in use at that time, a century before the German Third Reich), forced marches, sicknesses and diseases—remains to this day one of the worst blemishes on American history. While it is pointless to compare the collective tragedies of one tribal group of people with another in attempts to determine who had it the worst in the vast scale of human suffering of the era, it is nevertheless impossible to overlook the 4,000 Cherokee dead and lost during their particular removal. A large tribe comprising seven clans and nearly sixty communities in parts of four states—North Carolina, Tennessee, Georgia, and Alabama—numbering about 17,000 people (with another two-to-three thousand already in the West in Arkansas and Missouri), the Cherokees were indeed a nation.

On the Way (1838-1839)

Rain Crow

Assistant to the Reverend Jesse Bushyhead,
a wagon train contingent leader

Sgé! Listen!
A spavined horse stands beside the rutted road.
Wagons with busted axles
are hub-deep in the frozen mud.
Morning campfires that give no warmth.
People huddle against the winter wind,
a constant gale, blowing on and on,
and there is no surcease of pain and cold.
And off to the side of the frozen road
in a stand of leafless hackberries,
the five who died the night before
lie in stiffened attitudes
beside open graves (mouth of Mother Earth
black and pitiless, cold
and waiting — end for all our pains.)
And three who died not even three years old.

       Rain Crow speaks:
"Somebody said that seven children
were down this morning with whooping cough.
That makes eighteen now — not counting the
ones that died."
People in blankets stand waiting,
praying for the comfort that cannot be found,
waiting for the word to move on,
in another day of westward walking.
Wind howls like a wounded bear
filled with outrage.   Icicles
fall from naked branches
breaking into brittle slivers.
Over all the mantle of whiteness,
dotted with blackened forms of naked trees,
the expanse — and the way we — is illimitable.
        "Did you hear the wolves last night?
        If only the wind would stop."

Susie Wickham Speaks

Listen!
                    "It's hardest on the children
and the old folks."
Her son lies buried
back at Gunter's Landing.
She still has five more mouths
to feed and care for.
She stirs the kettle with a long stick
and dredges up the turnip greens,
picked frost-mauled two days ago
out of the inhospitable Arkansas ground.
                    "I can't ever stop thinking about it.
Them little faces all drawed up
in hunger and cold.
                    Some don't have shoes to wear, even."
The greens are ready.
She calls her family,
a poor breakfast,
but better than some folks will have.
                    "It's a pure-true trial on a body.
                    All our people ain't going to
make it. You know, a dead child
is a sure-hard fact to face."
In mortars of hewn log,
lives — like corn kernels —
are ground into a grain
of misery.

Only the buzzard knows
the watermark of our Evil Days.
Only the buzzard can claim
an ultimate authority.

Sudalidihi
Six Killer

Listen!
Sudalidihi had dreamt of green things,
Of unwinterlike things:
Tall green corn, and muskmelons,
Lying fat above the warm soil,
hidden in crisp weeds.
Scuppernongs on the vines,
trailing up hickories and sycamores.
Jaybirds and woodpeckers
making loud noise
in rhododendron thickets,
and whippoorwills calling softly
in the evening shade
of red haw and dogwood.
It was Green Corn Dance time in eastern Tennessee.
Cherokee men played the little war
on the ball-play field,
using racquets like war-clubs,
and bets were wildly made.
Then the young women played ball,
no less violently than the men.
Oconuluftee people had come over
to join the people of Chota town
for the summer holiday.
An outsider, a half-white Chickasaw,
had won the footrace
and his wife's people were happy.
        The dogs had jumped a fat buck
out of the tall corn.
The young men began the chase,
and the deer ran fast.
The people laughed and shouted,
cries echoed in the piney hollows
of the high hills.
The older men laughed softly, wisely,
as though to say:

You can't catch the wind.
The chase was not long:
when the buck reached the creek bank
and swam across,
the young people gave it up
and stopped,
and caught their breath
and played in the water.
Drops of splashing water
glistened in the sun and shade,
reticulate as a rattlesnake's back,
and the long hot summer sun
sank behind a hog-back ridge.
              A melting icicle awakens Sudalidihi.
Groaning, he remembers where he is.
His ninety years burdensome,
like old unmelting snow,
and they lay heavily
upon the earth of his flesh.

Going Snake

Listen!
Old, determined Going Snake,
rides his horse at eighty-two,
looking straight ahead and never back,
straight into the face of death,
straight to the west.
The young warriors follow him,
riding straight and proud,
tall as old-time Indians,
behind the Keeper of the Old Ways.

Siah Black Fox Broods

Head medicine man of the Catawba Creek settlement,
15 miles from the Georgia state line.
He is Bird Clan and uncle to Wilford Black Fox.

The black seed moved.
It moved
and I know I will not live out
this year of hardship.
It doesn't matter
knowing I am going to die.
But I am troubled by the thought
of my bones lying in a strange land —
far away from the bone-ground
that made them.
The old people have always said:
bones should return to earth
that made them
like rainwater returning
to clouds.

Tsali
Charley

Long ago
Tsali
man of the People
hid himself
and his family
in the pine–covered
hills of the old country.
Tsali died
and his sons
and his brother
in front of
a firing squad.
Tsali died,
but some of the people
got to remain
in the Carolina hills,
their homeland.
Through them,
you know now,
that the People,
at least some of them,
always remain
in the homeland.

Life-Everlasting

There is a flower   brown in its
texture   malleable as willow   old.
It blooms eternal
like old photographs   browning
in family cedar chests
the crackle of crisp paper   smell of
old flower residue   old   old.
Only eyes are young   and smiles
the high-button shoes   whale-bone stays
button collars   iron-hard as Puritan
law   to fall in love with such images
of ones who made the walk.

Earlier Times

Dragging Canoe Speaks, May 1775
Tsiyu-gun-siní

There is this land:
you will call it Transylvania.
There is this land:
you will call it home.
There is this land:
you will call it bluegrass.
There is this land of cane and green rivers
of savannas and salt licks,
buffalo herds, brown bears,
of warpaths and sulphur bogs
deer tame as your cattle
for not knowing a *yoneg* rifle shot.
There is this land of no man's land:
  Not Chickasaw, not Shawnee,
not Delaware, not Wyandot,
and not even Cherokee.
There is this land you will call by a strange name
the words a twist of our tongue
and nearly unknowable to us
in later years.
If you take this land from us
as you feel you must
you will find it a troubled land
a dark and bloody ground.
both our bloods will make it so
but yours more so than ours
will make it *ganda-giga-ii*
which you will call in later years:
  Kentucky.
There is this land.

This World

There are two worlds beyond This World
This one we know and live on
at present.
One is a chasm   framed between a gorge
and rocks below this one we stand on now.
The other is above us   beyond the Sky Vault
far beyond our seeing   but not so far
as Where the Dog Ran bands
the summer sky.

Look closely   you will see the world
I know is not the world you know.
My design of it   made on skins
of animals   will not work its mark
on most humans.

But for *Jilagí*
it will do.

Yonvlonohi

Sgé!
Listen!
Yonvlonohi
Creator.
Yona do-da (eyi) sv-na-li
Sun of other mornings.
Tsv-yawi-do-sdadiniyotli.
Have some goodness for your children.
Tadeya eh-sta-te kuhi.
Until we meet again.
Equo-ni un-e sta lv.
There will be icy rivers.
Ani-yon-wiyatla-no si-wu.
And you, Sun, will be no more for us.
Sgé!
Listen!
Yonvlonohi.
Creator.
Wi-do-sdaos-da ani-tsa-la-gi-yi.
Know we are all your good Cherokees.
Wado.
Thank you.
Wado.
     Thank you.
Wado.
          Thank you.
Wado.
             Thank you.

Sgé.

White Path, the Storyteller, Explains the Origin of the World
With respect to James Mooney

I will now tell you how this world was made.
We are on a great island
floating in a sea of water
suspended at each of the four cardinal points
by a cord from the Sky Vault,
which is made of solid rock.
    When the world grows old and worn out,
the People will die
and the cords will break.
The earth will sink into the ocean.
All will be water again.
We Indians are afraid of this,
but we are taught that we can
keep all intact
with special forms of conduct.
    When all was water
the animals were above in *Galún-latí,*
beyond the Sun's arch,
it was very crowded up above
and more room was needed.
The animals and humans
wondered what was below the water.
At last, *Dayu-nisi,* Beaver's Grandchild,
the little Water-beetle,
volunteered to find out what he could.
He darted, in the water,
in every direction
over the water's surface
and saw no firm place to rest.
Then *Dayu-nisi* dived to the bottom
and came back with some soft mud.
The mud then grew.
It grew and grew,
spreading one every side
until it became the island
which we Cherokees call the Earth.

It was then fastened to the sky
by four cords,
but no one remembers who did this.
    At first, the Earth was flat
and very soft and wet.
The animals were anxious to get down
so they sent out different birds
to see if it was dry enough,
but they found no place to light
and all came back to *Galún-latí*.
    At last it seemed to be time
so they sent out the Buzzard
and told him to make things ready.
This was the Great Buzzard,
the father of all the buzzards we see now.
He flew all over the Earth
in every direction
low down to the ground
and the ground was still soft.
When he reached the Cherokee country,
he was very tired.
His wings began to flap slower
and strike the ground
in his coursing.
Whenever his wings struck the Earth,
there was a valley scooped out
and when they turned up again,
there was a mountain.
When the animals above in *Galún-latí*
saw all this,
they were afraid the whole world
would be mountains,
so they called the Great Buzzard
to come back.
    And so the Cherokee country
remains full of mountains
to this day.
And also, children, listen to me now—
you should never kill a buzzard.

The Great Buzzard made our world,
not just the one we are leaving now,
but the whole world around us,
and he guards it to this day,
keeping us safe from sickness,
from the taint of all things dead.
Take care of him
As you would care for one another.

Little Deer

Her mother, Pigeon Woman, speaks

Another morning
and you are still with us.
I thank the Creator for it.
I wish you would eat.
It's been five mornings now
and you have not taken food.

The wolves were calling last night.
We are Wolf Clan people
and ought not to fear them,
but we do.

Your father is here.
He wishes you well and gives you his love.
Your two brothers are here,
and your aunts and your cousins — all
are here.
Know that you are not alone.

Our good medicine people
are doing all they can.
You will leave us soon, I know.

High up along the hillside
another medicine maker walks.
It is Rain Crow —
singing softly his songs of curing
for all our old and sickness-stricken.
I know he has words for you, too.

The wind, and now the snow,
torments us.
Your eyes no longer see me,
although you keep them open.
Know that I and all of us
love you.

Ohh, my little one, ohhh Creator,
now you have left us.
Go, my *usti,* go on your way west.
I know we will soon follow you.
Go, little one. Go, Little Deer.

President Van Buren

In his 1838 State of the Union Address, President
Martin Van Buren said the Cherokees had now emigrated
to their new home west of the Mississippi River
in Indian Territory, all with "the happiest
effects" and that it had all been accomplished
"without any apparent reluctance" on their part.

Of course, Van Buren never personally went to
their homeland in the Southeast, and certainly
not to their new home in Indian Territory, during
the removal era. His address was almost a year
before the Trail of Tears itself was undertaken—
whereby approximately one-fourth of the enrolled
16,000-plus tribal members either died or disappeared
during the winter march, but even before then,
many hundreds of people had already died
as a result of the homeland uprooting.
And this is not to mention the scores of other removed
Indians of the era. While he rejoiced over the
"happiest effects," the catastrophe of the winter death
march was already getting underway.

No wonder Martin Van Buren is considered one of the
most mediocre, if not worst, presidents, of all time.

Emerson Has Words for the President

Right after Chicken Snake's successor,
Martin Van Buren, in his 1838 State of the Union address,
a year after assuming the presidency,
sought to assure the American public
that the Cherokees had "happily" accepted
their removal to Indian Territory
and were at that very moment making their way
to the new land,
Ralph Waldo Emerson addressed
a public letter to him, in which he sought
to take the blinders off the eyes of the American public.
In highly respectful language, Emerson nonetheless
targets Van Buren's superficial reportage.
Van Buren either knew of the suffering Cherokees
were undergoing at the time
and had determined to make a smooth-over remark of it
or he was abysmally ignorant of the matter.
Either way, he is seen as not only a dimwit,
but also a sub-par president.

Emerson's letter points out the elements
of tragedy which the people were living
at the time   as well as
the remarkable humanity of the people,
thus further adding to the supreme
standing he holds not only in literature,
but also in American life and thought.

On the Way (1838-1839)

Richard Old Field Speaks

Listen!
On the twenty-eighth day of our going forth,
six days short of Nashville, Tennessee,
the long incessant days of rain turned to snow.
Who could have believed such wetness
after that long dry brush-fire summer
in the stockades?

Oxen grow lean, feeding off moss and tree bark
as government-promised grain was slow in coming.
I'd watch the slow steps of animals, of people,
grow slower still, as the rutted road got deeper.
The contingents behind — somebody told me
there are two or three more — will have it much harder
than us   trying to go over our ruts.
Today, more deaths reported.
That makes — too many!
Do we count the ones that ran away —
people returning to our homeland?
Do we count them as among the dead?

I watch Dirt Seller's boy — a thoughtful twelve-year-old
trying in these hard times to hurry up
and get grown   hustle out to the sides of the road
gathering dry grass and tree leaves and willow shoots
to off-set the tree-bark-eating of the overworked
oxen and horses
all the while talking to them in Cherokee.
I wonder, though I have a map in front of me,
how much longer? How much further?
And who will be the next to die?

Day Follows Day

Day follows day
and still the sky darkens.
The sun is cloud-hidden.
High winds blow but fail
to sweep the cloud banks eastward
though soon a southern breeze
warming in its reaching
sudden and random
moves a mass of clouds away
and then the sun   like a firelight
shines through
and then   just as sudden
more clouds move in.
The land is once more darkened
wind wails through treetops
bare as Christian gravestones
echoing the anguish of
a banished people
suffering, but bent on survival
and full of waiting
for an end of journeying
and of exile.
                    Blue north
                        Black west
                            White south
                                Red east
We pray
since prayer is what we know
and are.

George Lowrey Speaks

It's a fine time to be doing it,
I know, but this morning
I find I've had old Chicken-Snake Jackson
on my mind.
I was remembering that last meeting
we had with him   and him talking to us
like we were a bunch of
school-boys that he had
to correct for our own good.
Him, certain that he knows
what is best for us
simply because he was
a white man
and we were all Cherokees.

Quatie

There is a grave in Little Rock.
Beneath it lie the remains
of Quatie Ross
good Cherokee woman.
Beloved Woman like those of the old days.
She gave her blanket to a sick child
pellagra-stricken and suffering from cold.
The child lived, but Quatie Ross
died of pneumonia and toil.
She was the wife of Chief John Ross
and she left behind her a loving husband
and four children
and the love of her entire people.

Amá Agoshti Speaks
Dreadfulwater

You goddamned son-of-a-bitch—
you are as welcome among
us Cherokees
as a throat cut with a rusty knife.

Fact is, that's just what
I ask *youvlonohi*
have happen to you.
I only ask now
for your own good
that you stay away from my house
and my kind.
My knife is thirsty
and not so dull and rusty either.
Today you stand before us
unmasked
as the chicken-snake you are,
snake-head bastard that you are.

But all of this
is all in the manner
of how white men curse.
Let me curse you now
as an Indian would.
So:
May you enjoy yourself
washing your face in
ripe dog vomit,
and make your breakfast
on fresh cat feces.
I would also have maggots
infest your clothes and person.
And all other forms of excreta
I would wish attached to you.
Let me be more specific:
may fleas and ticks and lice
and mosquitoes and bedbugs and crabs

be your constant companions.
May the air you breathe be
forever befouled with your
ever-growing chronic halitosis,
like two-week-old dead dog flesh.
And may you know an eternity
of the seven-year-itch.
In all the forms of offal that
I wish for you to revel in,
the bottom line is this:
I wish you to stink to the
highest reach of your white man's heaven
so that your fellow *yonegs* will not come
within fifty miles of you.
then, in your exile,
you will know genuine loneliness,
the loneliness of one
against all things.
No friends.
Alone.
This is the worst of all earthly things.
This is our *Jilagí* way of swearing.

The Reverend Jesse Bushyhead Speaks

The crack of ice in trees
fills the air
like *unega* rifles on a massacre morning.
The wail of torture ascends
the frozen waste.
People, animals, covered wagons —
entire wagon trains —
stop at the Mississippi crossing-point:
the river is frozen solid.

Many two-voiced prayers aspire above the misery:
— Rock of Ages
cleft for me,
let me hide
myself in Thee . . .

O Lord God Jehovah in Heaven on High,
grant solace to your children.
Help us through this day
as you have helped us
for so many days gone by.
In Jesus' name, Father,
we ask Thy blessing.
Amen.

Listen! Ancient Red One,
Great Spirit,
Sun of other mornings,
make these bad times bearable.
Have a kindness on our little ones
and on all our old folks.
We suffer and we die
unless You melt this river's ice
and let us go forth,
we Cherokees will be no more.
So, listen, Ancient Red One,
Great Spirit,
have a kindness on your children,
we are all your good Cherokees.
Wado.
Sgé.

Crowfoot Speaks
James Crawford

The not-so-old   the unwise
the lame and the lost.
"Medicine-maker, make me well.
Undo all the bad medicine
put on me by some *sgíli*
from the outside flat country."
So speaks James Crawford (Crowfoot)
asking   believing   while not wanting
to believe   the power of *Jilagí* medicine
on this particular night—
cold and windy   with no clouds above.
The stars in the Belt of Orion
shine brighter than ever
like white rocks in a
cold dark mountain stream
in a moon-filled night.
And so Crowfoot waits.

In the New Land

Wilford Blackfox

Here, we are finally making it into
Indian Territory — or as the government agent
says, "Cherokee Nation."
Interesting country. Somewhat hilly, like back home —
oh, how them words — back home — torture me.

Uncle Siah, teaching me as much about medicine
as he could, is no longer with us.
He knew all along he wudn't gonna make it.
But I will try to do all the things he said
he wanted to do — to make sure our children
have a good chance to live after they come
into this country, how they can grow up big
and strong, how to find food where a
person might not expect it to be.
Lots of things, he said.
He showed me how sassafras works,
Jerusalem oak, different kinds of tobacco,
yarrow — aww, a whole lot of things.
How to watch for fleas and ticks and stop
the awful things they do to a body.
But I worry, too, not enough things do I know.
He reminded me to work with the ladies,
them child-birthing ones, how your health
has to start right at the very beginning, when
you're born. Medicine ladies, who say the
first four days of a person's life is the main
thing to get you started to have a good and strong
and healthy life. I hope I have learned it, but
I worry like heck that I ain't.

But I'll just keep remembering you, Uncle Siah,
and hope that will carry me along.

Aji-Náhsay
1895

The outlaw Briscoe Fields, finding himself
on the scout
far away from Cherokee Nation
and in the stick-and-mud town
of Chika-asha — "over-there town" —
now called Chickasha,
as the *Ani-Chikasa* call it.

Briscoe, a *Jilagí* without clan —
Aji-Náhsay — took his absences
from his homeland at first lightly,
but later as a troublesome burden.

Robbing banks   particularly in
Jilagí Nation   was not acceptable,
even though he had seen the
Bill Cook Gang and Yuchi bandit Rufus Buck
and his guys   and how they made out.
At least for a little while.
Even though he claimed that he only
robbed *yoneg* banks   still the Nation didn't
approve   and wanted posters
advertised the fact   declaring him a
non-*Jilagí*.
On his way to Mexico
he was shot and killed by a
Yoneg Texas Ranger
and buried in an unmarked grave,
the burden of being
Aji-Náhsay.

Charley Goings Holds Court

"Well, I guess the grass stopped growing,
and the water stopped running."
This is old Charley Goings,
grandson of Going Snake
who was speaker of the council
in the time of evil days.
His words seem to catch the echo
of other words   spoken long ago
to apparently no one in particular
but the wind   which always listens.
He is seated next to Martin Rattlinggourd
on a worn oaken bench on the porch
of the dry goods store.
There is also Tom Bearmeat and John Deerinthewater,
on another bench.
All old men   survivors of that long walk—
that *nunna da-ul tsunyi* —
the Road Where the People Cried.
They were children then
and now are old men,
sitting as old men are accustomed to doing
quietly honoring the mid-morning sunlight
of an early autumn morning.
The Oklahoma hills are noted
for their dry winds
whistling through scrub-oak gullies
and near-empty streets of small towns.
"Tonight's a Keetoowah night,"
Martin Rattlinggourd says   and
looks down the small town street   where
the statue of Stand Watie
overlooks the Tahlequah square
catching the rays of the coppery sun.
"What good'll a Keetoowah meeting be,
now, if that Dawes gut-eater
comes back here again?" Charley says.

"Oh, he'll be back. No need to worry none
about that," Tom Bearmeat says
and the others nod in agreement.
"Well, we ought to all just hide in the hills.
Let him look his tail off for us."
The men laugh quietly in a rolling collective chuckle.
And so do the younger ones   those
standing inside the store   all at
a respectful distance
from the old men who do the talking—
young Buck Gulager, the Lacy brothers Pick and Ed,
Elijah Rogers, Matthew Fields,
and the Creek boy Kaliedja Harjo,
visiting from over at Tulsy-town.
"It looks like it might be a
good night to go over to Arkansas,"
Buck Gulager says.
"Fort Smith across the line
drinking red-eye whisky in the white man taverns
and that government man
searchlighting the Cooksons,
trying to sign up Indians
to allotments they don't want."
Their quiet laughter drifts down
the leaf-strewn street
borne on breezes as unsettling
as their fears for tomorrow.

Robert Duck
History teacher, Sallisaw Public Schools

What does the Trail of Tears
mean for us today —
a century and a half later —
since that time of death and walking?
Well, to me, it means that so long
as there's a bigger government —
their good intentions and nice wishes to the contrary —
they will always do their damnedest
to make you do
what they want you to do —
and most of the time saying
it's all for your own good.
And the Christians are the worst —
and I'm a Christian, too,
but I'm an Indian first —
they know without question
that all that is best for themselves
is always also the best for you.
Anytime a Baptist preacher
Or a Catholic priest
sits down to talk with an Indian medicine maker
— if they ever do so
in the first place —
they will always feel themselves superior
and never on an equal footing.
So I say, it's always best to keep with one's own.
Listen, if you have to —
to these gut-pickers —
even nod your head occasionally,
but keep only the counsel
of your own kind.

Meeting Andrew Jackson in an Albuquerque Bar

I almost fell off the barstool when I saw him
coming from the pool room last night
ash-gray hair the color of an old fox's back
a pool cue in hand   like the militia saber
he used on the Creeks.

A little too loud   and much too quickly
I said to him   like a fool   "You
son-of-a-bitch. What about Horseshoe
Bend   Dancing Rabbit Creek   The Trail
of Tears
and what about that string of dead
Seminole towns   all along the forgotten
Florida backlands?"

He looked at me   like the bar-drunk
I guess I was   for the longest time
he held the pool cue poised   I waited
for the blade to fall   to see my trail of blood
lost in the history of the bar's cracked floor.

But he just glared at me   an old stern father look
with crazy Tennessee eyes
that sentenced me to walk a thousand miles
to a new land of shame.

And then I spoke again
old wily rabbit
though bent on survival
yet out to trick the fox
I said
"I am a man, and you are another."
He turned and stalked out the door
but I still see the saber leaning against
the bar   blood-caked and anachronistic
there for all to know
a thing to marvel at
a thing to revile.

Jonah Rollins Speaks

I am the son of
a son of sons of
Cherokees
in untold numbers.
       (There is this land.)
I bear witness
to a world of
pain and trouble.
I, poor fool,
born in the wrong time,
victim of a present
that hurries by
too quickly.
       (There is this land.)
On cold brittle mornings
as vees of geese
honk overhead,
I smell the blood
of history
in the winds of
change.
       (There is this land.)
My heart is mournful
as thunder
moving slowly across
distant hills
late on a long
still
warm
night of early autumn.
       (There is this land.)

Homeland

For M. K. J.

The hills are indeed red here.
And old, too.
Here, at a corner Chevron station
on one of Decatur's busiest streets
we wait for our ride to Emory.
I am vexed with myself
for forgetting to bring tobacco.
Instead, I take a small clod
of red clay
damp from the morning rain.
I hand you a part of it
while I keep the rest.
I feel our grandmothers'
And grandfathers' bones and flesh in it.
I breathe
And silently say
Yonvlonohi . . . (Creator)
Only a single word.
We are home.

Glossary

Cherokee names, as they are used today after translation into English, often reveal modernization, or English-American contact, in a fairly standardized way. For example, most pre-Christian/pre-American Cherokee names—such as Dreadfulwater (today) or Dreadful Water (earlier)—generally follow this format. Pre-Americanization: Rain Crow, Black Fox, Old Field, etc., become Raincrow, Blackfox, Oldfield, etc. Sometimes the names have modern variants: Going Snake (Goings), Crow Foot (Crawford), etc.

"Susie Wickham Speaks": The buzzard is a very special being for Cherokees.

"Sudalidihi":Green Corn Ceremonialism is very special to Cherokees, and all other Southeastern Indian tribes. In its original form as a four-day celebration in mid-summer, it was (is) a combination of New Year's, Christmas, Thanksgiving, and the Fourth of July all rolled into one.

"Going Snake": Going Snake was a real person, a traditional leader both before and after the Trail of Tears was completed.

"Siah Black Fox Broods": Black is a deeply symbolic color for Cherokees. It is the color of death (and the west), the opposite of red (the east), birth, life.

"Tsali":Tsali (Charley) was a real person.

"Dragging Canoe": The great 18th Century war chief, who fought invaders into his tribal homeland until his death in 1792. The naming of Kentucky by him is not universally agreed on. As well, there is a difference of opinion about his name. Many claim that with his death, it was the end of his family name among the Cherokees. I disagree. I contend that those today with the name of Otterlifter are his descendants. Otter-Canoe (atop the water) and Dragging-Lifting are virtually the same verb.

"This World": *Jilagí*—a form of *Tsalagi*; used by some Arkansas Cherokees.

"Where the Dog Ran" is a Cherokee name for the Milky Way.

"Galan-lati" is the traditional Cherokee homeland.

"Little Deer": *Usti* is little one, in Cherokee.

"George Lowrey": George Lowrey was Second Chief to John Ross, the Principal Chief during and after the Removal.

"*Amá Agoshti*": a version of the modern name Dreadful Water; some say it is a portion of water to be respected, even feared—like a whirlpool, or a river "suck."

A clanless person; a slave; an anomaly; a person without place or status within the Cherokee Nation, although their blood, if not heritage, might be of the people. Many Cherokees maintain that being born of Cherokee blood does not make one a Cherokee, but that one must be educated as one.

In traditional Native ways of cursing someone, to call them a "bastard" or a "son of a bitch," doesn't carry opprobrium since a person has no way of changing or reconciling one's origin. However, to allude to one's lack of personal hygiene, or physical lack of cleanliness (an aspect of the failure to "go to the water," for one thing), or one's undue rudeness or unmannerly conduct to someone yet unknown to them, all counts as human failing—in effect, it bespeaks an aspect of exile.

"*Yonvlonvhe*": a Cherokee version of the Creator; the Great Spirit.

"The Reverend Jesse Bushyhead": A real person. For most Cherokees, he represents an embodiment of the melding of traditional Cherokee ways with Christianity. This is reflected in his name as it is written: Bushyhead, instead of Bushy Head. *Sgili* is "witch" in Cherokee.

"Aji Náhsay": *Yoneg* is a modern slang version of *Unaka*, or *Uneka*; white person. *Ani Chikasa"* is "Chickasaw people" in Cherokee.

"Charley Goings Holds Forth": Cooksons (Cookson Hills)—a hill range in Northeastern Oklahoma.

Geary Hobson is a retired professor of English at the University of Oklahoma. His areas of teaching and scholarship are Native American literature, American literature and American Studies, and creative writing. He taught at the University of Oklahoma from 1988 to 2016.

He is the author of a novel, *The Last of the Ofos* (2000), a book of poetry, *Deer Hunting and Other Poems* (1990), the editor of the anthology, *The Remembered Earth: An Anthology of Contemporary Native American Literature* (1979), the co-editor of *The People Who Stayed: Southeastern Indian Writing After Removal* (2010), and a collection of short stories, *Plain of Jars and Other Stories* (2011). He has published poems, fiction, critical essays, and book reviews in more than one-hundred magazines and anthologies.

Of Cherokee and Quapaw/Chickasaw ancestry, he has been involved in Native literary studies and teaching for more than forty years, as well as with several national Native American literary organizations. In 2003, he received the Lifetime Achievement Award from the Native Writers' Circle of the Americas. He lives in Norman, Oklahoma.

Janet Lamon Smith, (*Nv Tse*, "one who walks about as in spirit") was a Cherokee artist who painted in the Baconian Traditional Style taught by Acee Blue Eagle, Dick West, and Ruthe Blalock Jones. Her paintings depicted the traditions, myths, and history of her tribe.

Janet was born in Tahlequah, Oklahoma to John and Lucille Lamon on May 14, 1943 and graduated from Okay High School in 1961. Mrs. Smith attended Bacone College, (Muskogee, OK), earned her BFA at from Northeastern State University (Tahlequah) and a Master's degree from Emporia State University (KS). Smith worked as an Art Therapist with Cherokee Nation and Indian Health Services. She received many awards and accolades for her work in Art Therapy and as a Native American Artist. Janet and was an active member of the Wagoner and Okay communities.

Janet Lamon Smith passed away on January 3, 2020. Following her wishes, Mongrel Empire Press honored this great loss to her tribe, her friends and family, and the Native arts community by donating to Wagoner Community Outreach and by planting a tree in her name through the American Forests Organization.